LENT COURSES
FROM KEVIN MAYHEW

The first chapters from five new and bestselling courses
to help you choose the best one for your community

First published in 2006 by
KEVIN MAYHEW LTD
Buxhall, Stowmarket, Suffolk, IP14 3BW
E-mail: info@kevinmayhewltd.com
www.kevinmayhewltd.com

9 8 7 6 5 4 3 2 1 0

ISBN 1 84417 708 4
Catalogue No. 1500965

Cover design by Sara-Jane Came

Contents

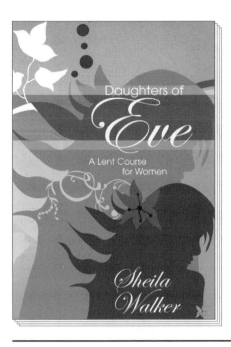

Daughters of Eve

A Lent Course for Women
Sheila Walker

Catalogue No:	1500947
ISBN:	1-84417-689-4
Price:	£4.99

What does a godly woman look like in the twenty-first century? In a time and culture where roles are continually changing, lines of demarcation are blurring and fashion is often unisex, there is a pressing need for today's daughters of Eve to do the three things this group Lenten course sets out to achieve:

- To look at the challenges, opportunities and temptations of each of the 'five ages of woman'

- To reflect on the experience of being one of those five ages

- To see what the Bible has to say to help all daughters of Eve live out their spiritual potential

Each of the five sessions (with an optional sixth) uses prayer, scripture, discussion and action (!) to reflect upon a different age period in the cycle of a woman's life to bring a greater insight into their own lives and their place within the communities of which they are a part.

Many of the issues raised in this book will relate equally to men!

Session 1: Up to 18ish

Discovering

Pray

Two prayers are provided: the first for those in this age group; the second for those who are older. Choose either or both, depending on the make-up of your group.

Prayer 1

> Father in Heaven, thank you for all that is good about being a young person growing up today, and for your help in all the things that can be difficult.
>
> Please help me to understand myself, and my own generation; may I then be able to help others in my church to understand us better, and how we can contribute to their lives; help me to understand, too, how their wisdom and experience can help us, so that we all grow together as a family.
>
> I ask this in the name of your Son, Jesus Christ – who was once a child and a teenager. Amen.

Prayer 2

> Father in Heaven, thank you for all that was good about my own childhood and teenage years: and thank you for bringing me through all the times that were difficult.
>
> Please help me to reflect on that time, and understand what was significant, and relevant for today; may I be able to share those things graciously, to help the young people in my church. Help me to learn from them about the issues they face, and about the gifts they have to offer me, so that we all grow together as family.
>
> I ask this in the name of your son, Jesus Christ – who was once a child and a teenager. Amen.

Today

Choose one or more of the following activities to 'earth' your reflections.

1. If you have young people in your group, encourage them to bring a typical teenage magazine (whether or not they usually read it, and not a Christian one). If not, buy one – your local newsagent will tell you what's popular, if you're not sure! Give everyone a few pages, and time to have a look at them: then share your thoughts about what kind of 'diet' this is for our young people.

2. Who watches which soaps? How are children and young people portrayed in them? Is this fair? Spend a few minutes sharing your observations.

3. Make a quick sketch of a 'typical teenager today' (either individually or together). Why have you included each detail? How is it significant? *Is* it typical?

What *Did* God Say?

Looking up 'teenager' in a Bible concordance is pretty much a waste of time. Why? But *are* the issues so very different now?

You may like to compare the following passages in different versions of the Bible; these are from *The Message* (which Dr Jim Packer described as 'a blend of accurate scholarship and vivid idiom'). The first is from Proverbs – that utterly down-to-earth manual of wisdom for daily living – then *and* now?

> *Start with God – the first step in learning is bowing down to God;*
> *only fools thumb their noses at such wisdom and learning.*
> *Pay close attention, friend, to what your father tells you;*
> *never forget what you learned at your mother's knee.*
> *Wear their counsel like flowers in your hair,*
> *like rings on your fingers.*
> *Dear friend, if bad companions tempt you,*
> *don't go along with them.*
> *If they say – 'Let's go out and raise some hell.*
> *Let's beat up some old man, mug some old woman.*
> *Let's pick them clean*
> *and get them ready for their funerals.*
> *We'll load up on top-quality loot.*

We'll haul it home by the truckload.
Join us for the time of your life!
With us, it's share and share alike!'
Oh, friend, don't give them a second look;
don't listen to them for a minute. Proverbs 1:7-15

The second is from Jeremiah, a prophet who lived through agonisingly difficult times but held true to God's call to him when he was only young.

'Before I shaped you in the womb,
I knew all about you.
Before you saw the light of day,
I had holy plans for you:
A prophet to the nations –
that's what I had in mind for you.'
But I said, 'Hold it, Master God! Look at me.
I don't know anything. I'm only a boy!'
God told me, 'Don't say, "I'm only a boy."
I'll tell you where to go and you'll go there.
I'll tell you what to say and you'll say it.
Don't be afraid of a soul.
I'll be right there, looking after you.'
God's Decree.
God reached out, touched my mouth, and said,
'Look! I've just put my words in your mouth – hand-delivered!
See what I've done? I've given you a job to do . . .' Jeremiah 1:5-10a

Have Your Say

Look again at the passage from Proverbs. Is **discovering** bound to be a matter
of trial and error?

1. How would young people today respond to verses 7-9? (You might like
   also to look up Leviticus 19:32; Psalm 119:9; Exodus 20:12.) Does our
   'post-modern' wariness of authority make things harder, or do young
   people always want to do things their own way? Did you? What if your
   parents are unreasonable and your local church is dead?

2. Verses 10-15 have a very contemporary ring! Maybe girls are less likely to
   be persuaded to beat someone up: but what are the temptations for them

to go with the flow, be one of the crowd? (See also Genesis 8:21; Psalm 25:7.) What can help in resisting these temptations? Look now at the passage from Jeremiah. In some ways, this is the other side of the coin: a word of encouragement.

3. At what age might God be at work in someone's life? How do we know? (Look at Mark 10:13-16; Luke 1:13-15; Psalm 139:13-16.) How should we respond?

4. What are the qualities of children and young people that might be especially pleasing to God? (Remember 1 Samuel 3:10; 2 Kings 5:2-3; also Luke 1:38 – Mary would have been a teenager: who said all teenage pregnancies were unwanted?)

Take Away

Here are some ideas for action points: ways in which we can build on what we are learning. You may well be able to come up with ones that are better suited to your own situation; the important thing is that **reflection leads to action**.

a. Henry James described the young as 'terrible little baffling mysteries'. Perhaps, if we're no longer in that age group, that's how they appear to us! How about asking someone in this age group 'What's the best thing about being your age? And what's the worst thing?' Resist the temptation to accept the generation gap.

b. **Adoption** need not always be a long, difficult process – it can take many useful forms! If you are a young person, is there an older person in your congregation or community who could be your adopted grandparent, and pray for you, write to you, provide you with opportunities to serve and care for them? Could the Mothers' Union or women's group 'adopt a child' from the crèche or Sunday club and pray for them and their family? Or a student on their way to university? Could older Christians mentor or adopt new, younger believers?

c. How about offering to help with Sunday club, crèche, youth group – if not as a leader, then to provide refreshments, transport, prayer, materials, help provide an event for parents? Resist the temptation to insist that 'young people aren't my thing'.

d. Are there particular issues relating to young people in your area? Why not ask someone from the local police, school, social services or medical centre to come and talk to your congregation about local issues and how the church might be able to help?

e. For older people: Who are the young people in your own family and friendship circle? When did you last contact them? Why not do it now? Maybe you could ask if there's anything they would like you to pray for them.

f. For younger people: If you feel unsure about God's work in your life, or if you lack confidence, resist the temptation to write yourself off! Instead, write out some of the verses above (e.g. from Jeremiah, Psalm 139) and pin them up in your room: keep on telling yourself the truth!

g. Are there particular children or young people you are concerned for? Why not meet up with a friend and pray for them on a regular basis?

h. Has anything emerged from this study which you should discuss with your church leader? Try to do it as soon as possible.

Pray Again

Spend some time quietly reflecting on what you have studied and shared, and thinking through how you would want to respond.

Under 18?

How can I best relate to, and encourage my friends to follow Jesus and resist the temptations to go with the crowd? How can I best relate to the older people in my church and community, learn from them and serve them?

Over 18?

How can I best keep in touch with the under 18s, to understand how I can encourage them and learn from them? Are there particular young people the Lord is asking me to care for and, if so, how?

Lord God,
when you first created your world, you saw that it was very good.
Now it is a right old mixture of good and bad,
all waiting to be discovered.

Lord, we pray for all of us, but particularly for those of us under 18:
keep us close to you, reading your word, listening for your Spirit
so that we will discern what is good, and follow it;
what is evil, and resist it.
Show us, too, how we can help and encourage one another:
teaching without dictating; learning and discerning;
guiding without smothering; earning, not demanding respect;
listening, obeying, growing in the power of your Spirit
so that your Kingdom may come, and your will be done
in your power, and to your glory. Amen.

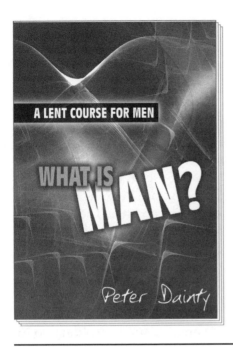

What Is Man?

A Lent Course for Men
Peter Dainty

Catalogue No:	1500961
ISBN:	1-84417-704-1
Price:	£4.99

What Is Man? is a Lent course for men with the main aim to consider how Christian men in the modern world can best serve God, and what the place of humanity as a whole is in the purposes of God. In other words, 'man' will be used in two senses in this course: to refer to individual males (man), and to refer to the whole human race (Man), male and female.

In the first four sessions, Peter Dainty looks at the place of Man on this planet and some of the responsibilities involved in daily life. Session five considers Man's weakness and mortality (sin, suffering and death) and how they affect our relationship with, and faith in, God. Session six looks at Jesus, the Son of Man, and asks what that title might mean.

The structure for each session is very simple and consists of three parts: Food for thought, Bible study and Closing prayer.

The sessions are:

- What is Man?
- The image of God?
- Man's responsibilities – work and rest
- Man's responsibilities – money
- Man's weakness and mortality
- The Son of Man

Session 1
What Is Man?

'What is man that thou art mindful of him, and the son of man that thou dost care for him?' asked the Psalmist (Psalm 8:4 RSV); or, if you want a modern version, 'What are human beings that you are mindful of them, mortals that you care for them?' (New Revised Standard Version – NRSV). These are big questions, and every generation asks them in one form or another. The Victorian music hall comic, Dan Leno, used to say, 'Ah, what is man? Wherefore does he why? Whence did he whence? Whither is he withering?'

Food for Thought

Plenty of people have been ready to answer such questions; so to stir up your own brain cells on these big issues, here are some random answers for you to consider and discuss. Ask yourselves how much truth they contain and in what way they are inadequate, and see if the Bible references throw any light on them.

a. Glory to Man in the Highest! For man is the master of things. *(Algernon Charles Swinburne, nineteenth-century English poet)* Isaiah 40:13-15; 45:9,13; Luke 2:14; Hebrews 2:6-8.

b. Man is 'a naked ape'. *(Desmond Morris, twentieth-century English zoologist)* Genesis 1:26-27; Romans 8:29; Colossians 1:15.

c. Man is but a reed, the weakest in nature, but a reed which thinks. *(Blaise Pascal, seventeenth-century French theologian and mathematician)* Psalm 139:23,24; Isaiah 40:6-8; Philippians 4:8.

d. Man is a 'degraded mass of animated dust'. *(Lord Byron, nineteenth-century English poet)* Genesis 2:7; Genesis 3:19; 1 Corinthians 15:45-50.

e. Man is what he eats. *(Ludwig Feuerbach, nineteenth-century German philosopher)* Matthew 4:4; John 6:27, 33-35.

Bible Study: What is man?

The question, 'What is man?' occurs three times in the Old Testament in slightly differing forms – Psalm 8:4, Job 7:17 and Psalm 144:3. We shall begin with Psalm 8 and come across the others later in the course (page 36).

Read Psalm 8

Note that the Psalmist is looking at the night sky (verse 3), and the sight of the moon and stars makes him aware of his own smallness and apparent insignificance. The Psalmist didn't know how far away the stars were, or the moon either for that matter. He didn't know about light years and galaxies and nebulae and black holes, or that some of those stars he saw were much bigger than our sun. He didn't know that there are probably billions of planets out there, which we are only just beginning to discover. He didn't know the distances which separate the planets in our solar system, or the even bigger distances which separate our milky way galaxy from the billions of other galaxies in the universe. He didn't know that even if you were able to travel at the speed of light (186,000 miles per second) it would still take you four and a half years to reach the nearest star to our sun – Alpha Centauri. It would take you much much longer to reach the nearest galaxy.

Does it concern you that we on this planet are so small in a vast universe?

Is God only concerned about big things? Discuss the way God uses small things and ordinary people to fulfil his purposes, both in creation and in human history.

If we look more closely at Psalm 8, however, we find that the Psalmist wasn't really concerned about the size of the universe or his own smallness in comparison; he simply wanted to praise the greatness of the Creator. This is his main theme from beginning to end – 'O Lord, our Lord, how majestic is thy name in all the earth!' he sings (verses 1 and 9, RSV). For he knew that it was

God who established the moon and the stars, and the heavens were the work of God's fingers (verse 3).

Contrast that faith in the Creator with these words of the French writer, Anatole France (1844-1924): 'What blows the mind is not the immensity of the star-filled heavens, but the fact that humans have been able to measure them.' It was that kind of attitude which no doubt influenced the 13-year-old schoolboy who wrote in an essay, 'I believe it was not God but science which created the universe.' They didn't seem to realise that the universe was there long before scientists started to investigate it. How did it get there? Who made the rules by which it works?

Do you think these are questions which science can ever answer?

The German astronomer, Johann Kepler was one of the pioneers of modern science in the seventeenth century, and a believing Christian. He had a friend who was an atheist and who tried to persuade Kepler that the universe came into being automatically by itself. So Kepler constructed a model of the solar system with the sun at the centre and the planets circling round it mechanically. When his friend saw it he exclaimed, 'What a marvellous model! Who made it?' Kepler answered, 'Nobody made it. It made itself.' His friend retorted, 'Nonsense. Somebody must have made it.' So Kepler replied, 'My friend, you think that this little toy could not make itself; yet it is only a poor imitation of part of the great universe that you say *did* make itself.' Whatever you make of Kepler's argument, no scientist or philosopher has been able to replace the idea of God as Creator with an idea which is more positive or inspiring.

The Psalmist was not only amazed by the greatness of God the Creator, he was also amazed by the fact that in spite of man's smallness, God still thought about him and cared for him, in fact he had given man a key role in his creation – the stewardship of planet earth (verses 5-8). Note that these verses are derived from the story of creation in Genesis 1, where God makes man in his own image and gives him authority to manage the earth (Genesis 1:26-28).

Throughout the twentieth century many people developed a view of the universe which didn't include God. This atheism resulted in a very pessimistic picture of man's life on earth. The French existentialist philosopher, Jean Paul Sartre, described human life as 'an empty bubble on a sea of nothingness'; the Irish artist, Francis Bacon, said that 'Man now realises he is an accident, that he is a completely futile being', and Bertrand Russell, the mathematician and philosopher wrote, 'Brief and powerless is man's life; on him and all his race the slow sure doom falls pitiless and dark.' Others began to describe human beings as nothing but walking bags of chemicals or biological computers, or a little mould on a grain of dust. Such is the world without God – empty of meaning, purpose and hope.

What else was going on in the twentieth century which might have encouraged such pessimism and atheism?

Discuss how belief in God gives hope and significance to human life on earth.

When the Church of Scotland minister, George Matheson, moved to his second post at Innellan, Argyleshire, he was horrified to feel that he had lost his faith in God and become an absolute atheist. 'I believed nothing,' he wrote later, 'neither God nor immortality. I tendered my resignation to the Presbytery, but to their honour they wouldn't accept it. They said I was a young man and would change. I *have* changed.' He stayed as a minister in Innellan for the next eighteen years, and then moved to Edinburgh until his retirement, all the time coping with very poor eyesight amounting to almost total blindness. He wrote the much loved hymn, 'O love that wilt not let me go', which sums up his own Christian experience in times of struggle and darkness. At times when he felt he had let go of God, he discovered that God had not let go of him.

Have you had any experience of faith/doubt which you would like to share with the group?

Closing Prayer

Lord of all worlds, we marvel at your creative power revealed in the magnificence of the heavens above and the mystery of life on earth. We wonder at that eternal love from which has flowed this amazing multiplicity of things – from atoms to galaxies, from dewdrops to oceans, from nodding flowers to twinkling stars, from sparking fireflies to blazing suns. We praise you for this out-pouring of your very self in the beauty, joy, light and life of the world, in the music of the spheres and the drama of universal history.

Creator of all things: **we praise your holy name.**

We thank you, Lord, for giving us faith – for putting a longing for you in our hearts. We thank you for all those experiences which have turned us towards your light, and opened our spirits to a sense of your living presence. For every word of truth, for every awesome feeling, for every soul-stirring emotion we give you thanks.

Creator of all things: **we praise your holy name.**

If ever we are lost in the darkness of doubt and fear, Lord, do not let us go. Stay with us through the night until the morning comes. Then give us a fresh vision; revive our confidence in your loving presence, and fill our hearts and minds with hope and peace. For without you we die, but with you we live.

Creator of all things: **we praise your holy name.**

Lord, when we observe the miracle of your creation, give us also the eyes of faith, with which to see the hidden meaning of it all – the love from which it springs and the goodness to which it moves – until all things are made one in you.

Creator of all things: **we praise your holy name,**
through Jesus Christ our Lord. Amen.

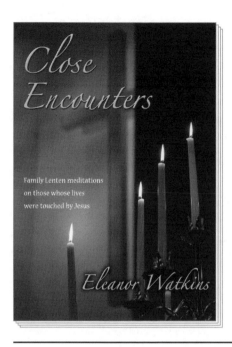

Close Encounters

Family Lenten meditations
on those whose lives were
touched by Jesus
Eleanor Watkins

Catalogue No:	1500962
ISBN:	1-84417-705-X
Price:	£6.99

Lent is a time to draw closer to Jesus, and to be touched by him. In this devotional Lenten book, Eleanor Watkins meditates upon the transforming personal encounters with Jesus recorded in the Gospels – from the big characters like Joseph and Peter, to the no less important little boy who had the five loaves and the two fish – and draws the reader into those encounters.

For each of the forty days of Lent there is a presentation of a different character accompanied by a reading, a reflection and a prayer.

Mary
Blessed among women

Day
1

The angel said: *'Greetings, Mary!'*

She said: *'Why have you come? I am afraid.'*

The angel said: *'Don't be afraid. You have found favour with God.'*

She said: *'I am just a young girl.'*

The angel said: *'You will have a son. He will be a mighty king and he will be called Jesus.'*

She said: *'How can this be? I'm not even married. I am a virgin.'*

The angel said: *'This will be God's son. Nothing is impossible to those who obey him.'*

She said: *'May the will of God be done.'*

Eleanor Watkins, Going with God, Kevin Mayhew 1999

Reading: Luke 1:26-38

We owe a great deal to Mary of Nazareth. A young girl, barely old enough to be married, living in a male-dominated society in an occupied land; yet God chose her to be the mother of the one who would bring redemption to a sin-sick world.

Mary was greatly troubled, both by the appearance of the angel and by the message he brought. If what he promised came true, the repercussions would be terrifying. Her pregnancy would bring shame to herself and her family, to Joseph, and to their community. Tongues would wag, fingers would be pointed and her reputation would be in tatters.

Yet Mary chose to believe God. She had an obedient childlike heart and put herself into the hands of her heavenly Father, understanding very little of what was to come. She trusted God and gave her consent to his plan.

What would have happened if she had been too frightened, too apprehensive, too overwhelmed to agree? Would God have raised up someone else to be the mother of his Son, or devised a plan B?

Maybe. But Mary said yes to God. She walked a step at a time in obedience to her Father, brought her child into the world, nurtured and loved him with a mother's joy as he grew to boyhood and then manhood, and saw her task through to the end.

Reflection: *Do we need to see a 'blueprint' before we can agree to God's purposes for our lives? Can we walk with him, a step at a time, trusting him to provide all we need to take the next step? Can we trust him enough to accept that there will be sorrow and hardship as well as joy in his plans for us, but that ultimately it will be 'turned into glory'?*

Prayer: *Lord, draw me so close that, like Mary, I will obey without question, knowing that all your ways are perfect.*

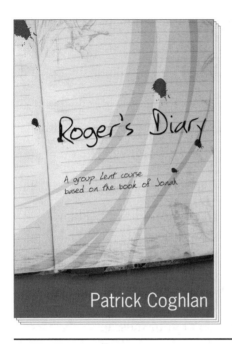

Roger's Diary

A group Lent course based on
the book of Jonah
Patrick Coghlan

Catalogue No: 1500963

ISBN: 1-84417-706-8

Price: £6.99

Roger's Diary is a series of imaginative and sometimes humorous resources to help groups prayerfully, reflectively and in the power of the Holy Spirit seek what God is saying to them through the book of Jonah.

The six sessions of this group Lent course look at the nature of God and how that affects our personal Christian journey:

- Called to serve
- Hard times
- Crying out to God
- A fresh start
- True repentance
- Loved and valued

Session 1*
Called to serve

Opening prayer

Loving Heavenly Father,
    open our ears
    to listen to what you are saying to us through Scripture,
    open our minds
    to understand what your word means to us today,
    open our hearts
    to receive and share your love with others,
    open our lips
    in praise, prayer and proclamation of your message,
    and let our lives reveal to others the person of Jesus.
Fill us afresh with your Holy Spirit,
    strengthen our faith and commitment to Christ,
    and be with us during this journey
    of enrichment and renewal.
In Jesus' name.
Amen.

Roger's diary

Characters   Roger Best, Nora Bone, Gladys Boottlethwaite, Jayne Harper, Bessie Ramshaw, Barry Smith, Sybil Smith, Michael Woods

Doesn't time fly? It was the Bible study group tonight. As usual, I arrived at the church hall quite early to give me the chance to get the chairs and Bibles out,

* See p.48 for extracts from 'Summary of sessions' and 'Extracts from Jonah's Journal'.

ready for when people arrived. Then, while I was looking at the notice board, something caught my eye. Fancy that still being pinned up there, I thought – a photograph of the church weekend away at the Old Mill House, down by the coast. It was a good weekend . . . but it must be nearly four years ago now. A lot has happened since then. The church has grown, spiritually and numerically. Some new folk have joined us and others have moved on. Anyway, I took down the old print and blew the dust off. It brought back some fond memories. I was miles away when Gladys Boottlethwaite arrived, early as usual, sporting a fresh blue rinse . . .

Gladys   [*Bangs the door*] Jack said he might come *next week* . . . so long as he's up to date with the garden!

Then curiosity got the better of her.

Gladys   What have you got there?

Roger   Oh, just remembering the time we went to the Old Mill House. Would you like to have a look?

Gladys frowned. I felt that she had never really appreciated what the weekend away had been about. The door of the church hall creaked open once again. Bessie Ramshaw and Nora Bone tiptoed in, both thinking that they were late. Gladys peered at her watch – just checking!

Roger   Is it still warm out there? I'll open the window, shall I? Let some air in.

Nora   If you like. It is warm for the end of June. Been a hot few weeks, hasn't it?

[The window creaks open]

Bessie   I have worked up a bit of a sweat walking up here. Sid used to love this weather. *[Thoughtful pause]* I do miss him.

Over the next few minutes, several others arrived to join in with the evening's study: Michael Woods, Sybil and Barry Smith and Jayne Harper.

Sybil   *[Enthusiastically]* I like your green hair, Jayne. It's . . . it's very . . . it's very you! And it goes well with your multicoloured dress – I've never seen those particular colours used together before.

Jayne   *[Casually]* I've been doing textile dyeing at college this week.

Gladys   *[Turning to Nora]* Nice tweed skirt, Nora. You dress so well . . . unlike some I could mention.

Michael   It's a good job we don't all like the same things; isn't it? It would be a very dull world.

Gladys   *[Irritated]* No fear of that!

Roger   Grab a chair, everyone, then we'll open in prayer . . . *[In a raised voice, over the noise of chairs being dragged]* We're going to start looking at the book of Jonah tonight – the first three verses of chapter one.

Michael read the short passage, slowly and clearly.

Barry   Wouldn't like to have been in Jonah's shoes.

Gladys   Not a lot to talk about there! When Reverend Hughes, your predecessor, was here we'd always cover at least a whole chapter in an evening.

Roger Thank you for that, Gladys. But you're wrong with your first comment: there's plenty to discuss – a God who calls, a God who has given us a message to share, a God of justice, and a God who has given us the freedom to make choices.

Sybil Praise the Lord!

Jayne Cool!

It was indeed an interesting evening. We investigated various questions: What is a calling? Why does God choose to use us in his plans? The nature of the message he wants us to share . . . and, of course, why did God give us free will? Especially when he knew how irresponsibly we would use it. We closed with a time of open prayer.

Nora Everyone want tea?

Jayne Any sparkling spring water?

Nora I'm sorry, dear, just tea, coffee or orange squash.

Barry No whisky, then?

Jayne I'll just have a cup of hot water, then, please.

Gladys I've brought some cherry buns that my domestic made today.

I'm not sure if it is politically correct to talk about domestics these days. But they were good buns . . . and that's how the evening ended.

Read

Jonah 1:1-3

Feelings plus

- In Jonah's position, what do you think might be going through your mind as you prepare your escape?
- Where has his reasoning gone wrong?
- What are the signs of people turning their backs on God in twenty-first century society?

Time of personal reflection

- God calls Jonah to go to Nineveh with a mission. Where has God placed you to serve him? What is God calling you to do? What talents and abilities has God given you? Whose lives does God want to touch, with his love, through you?
- Jonah is not willing to obey. Are you?
- It is a privilege to be part of God's plan for creation. How do you regard Christian service?
- The people of Nineveh have been guilty of terrible sins. We might feel that we have lived reasonable lives, but the reality is that we have all fallen short of God's standards in some way. Are there things in your life that are not honouring to God?
- How would you describe your relationship with God?

Time to share

Key verses

Jonah 1:

- Verses 1 and 2 – A God who calls
- Verse 2 – A God who wants to communicate with us
- Verse 2 – A God of justice
- Verse 3 – A God who gives us free will

Bible search

- Esther 4:12-14 – How does this passage illustrate that serving God is a privilege?
- Ezekiel 33:7 – Discuss the nature of a watchman. In what way are we called by God to be watchmen/women?[1]
- Matthew 5:13-16 – Jesus calls us to be salt and light. Give examples of how this could apply to life in the twenty-first century?
- Matthew 7:13-14 and Mathew 7:24-27 – Why do you think God has given us freedom of choice – in particular, the freedom to choose whether or not to follow Jesus and live God's way?
- Mark 1:15, John 14:6 and Romans 3:23, 24 – What do you understand to be the Christian message?
- Acts 1:8 – Jesus calls us to be his witnesses; and promises to empower us with the Holy Spirit. What does it mean to be a witness?[2]

---

[1] The task of the watchman is to sound the alarm, warning of approaching danger. It is a position of great responsibility.

[2] A witness is someone who shares from personal experience.

Prayer

Lord Jesus,
fulfil your plan in us today.

Thank you for dying on the cross for us all,
    paying the penalty for sin
    and providing the way to forgiveness, inner peace,
    spiritual healing and wholeness,
    so that our relationship with God may be restored,
    and we may live with the hope of eternal life in his presence.
Lord Jesus,
fulfil your plan in us today.

Thank you for wanting us to be your hands and feet,
    to do your work in the world around us today,
    to be salt and light in a broken world,
    to be your witnesses in a world that lacks hope,
    to be watchmen and women sharing the message of freedom
    and to share your love with others.
Lord Jesus,
fulfil your plan in us today.

You have called us to follow you.
Give us faith,
    and equip us and transform us through your Holy Spirit.
Lord Jesus,
fulfil your plan in us today.

You have called us to serve you:
    help us to respond willingly.
Lord Jesus,
fulfil your plan in us today.

You have given us the freedom to make choices:
    help us to choose wisely,

to distinguish right from wrong
and to discern your will in all things.
Lord Jesus,
fulfil your plan in us today.
Amen.

Opportunity for prayer ministry

Journal

Keep a journal of your personal response to this course.

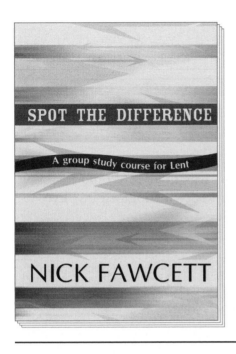

Spot the Difference

A group study course for Lent
Nick Fawcett

Catalogue No:	1500964
ISBN:	1-84417-707-6
Price:	£6.99

What difference does being a Christian make to your life and what difference should it make?

In *Spot the Difference*, Nick Fawcett considers five ways in which commitment should manifest itself: in a quality of love, a spontaneity of witness, a disposition of joy, a generosity of spirit and a vibrant inner faith.

The five sessions in this group study course for Lent are:

- A love that shows
- An allegiance that shows
- A joy that shows
- A concern that shows
- A faith that shows

Each session contains: Setting the scene, Activity, Exploring the Scriptures, Enlarging the picture, and Food for thought.

Session 1
A love that shows

Theme

The 'new commandment' of Jesus was that we should love one another, but how far does love actually distinguish our lives as Christians?

Opening prayer

O God of love, we ask you to give us love:
    love in our thinking,
    love in our speaking,
    love in our doing,
    and love in the hidden places of our souls;
    love of those with whom we find it hard to bear,
    and love of those who find it hard to bear with us;
    love of those with whom we work,
    and love of those with whom we take our ease;
    so that at length we may be worthy to dwell with you,
    who are eternal love.
Amen.
William Temple (1881–1944)

Setting the scene

Let love be the controlling force in your life, just as Christ loved us, giving himself up as a fragrant offering and sacrifice pleasing to God. (Ephesians 5:2)

The commandments 'You shall not commit adultery, shall not murder; shall not steal, shall not yearn for what belongs to someone else' – these and indeed all others – are encapsulated in a single command: 'Love your neighbour as yourself. If you love others, it stands to reason you will not wrong them; to love, in other words, is to obey the Law.' (Romans 13:9, 10)

Activity

Take a look at the pictures [on page 36]. Can you spot eleven differences between them? [The answers can be found on page 48 of this Lent Course Sampler.]

Talk together afterwards about what sort of differences there should be in the life of a Christian, and how far these ought to show.

Introduction

It's never easy to summarise something important in a few words, but with Christianity we're invited to do just that, and by none other than Jesus himself. For him all the commandments and everything God requires of us boil down to one thing: love. So, unsurprisingly, the New Testament writers have much to say on this theme, time and again emphasising the importance of love in any authentic discipleship; this, more than any other, is the central message of the gospel and the defining mark of God's people. Quite simply, as John reminds us, if we do not love then we do not know God – the two belong together. But do we love in a way that is any different to those around us? If asked to describe how your faith comes across to them, would anyone you know include love in their answer? The following passages bring home just how important a question that is.

Exploring the Scriptures

John 13:34, 35; 15:12

I give you now a new commandment: that you love one another. You must love each other just as I have loved you. If you have such love, people everywhere will recognise you as my disciples. This, then, is my commandment – that you love one another as I have loved you.

1 John 2:9, 10; 4:7-12, 20, 21

If we claim to be in the light but hate others, we are, in fact, even now in the darkness, but if we love others, then we live in the light, and nothing in us will lead others to sin. Dear friends, let us love one another, because love comes from God; all those who love are born of God and know God. Whoever does not love knows nothing of God, for God is love. God demonstrated his love like this – he sent his only Son into the world in order that we might live through him. In this is love, not that we loved God but that he loved us and sent his Son to be the expiation for our sins. Dear friends, given that God has loved us like this, shouldn't we love one another similarly in turn? Although no one has actually ever seen God, if we love one another, then he is one with us and his love is perfected in us. We cannot love him, whom we have never seen, unless we love others, whom we have seen. Christ's command to us is this: those who love God must also love others.

Prayer

Lord Jesus Christ,
   fill us, we pray, with your light
   that we may reflect your wondrous glory.
So fill us with your love
   that we may count nothing too small to do for you,

nothing too much to give,
and nothing too hard to bear.
Amen.
St Ignatius Loyola (1491–1556)

Enlarging the picture

To some, the Christian's talk of love is just wishy-washy idealism, a way of glossing over the need for moral decision-making, avoiding taking a stand on controversial issues. Loving one another, they say, is all very well, but what does it involve in practice? We need guidelines, rules, boundaries – clearly marked lines that spell out how love ought to show itself in specific situations.

Is that right? I can understand the concern, for love undeniably leads different people to act in different ways, what seems right to one seeming wrong to another. But is that not precisely the point of Jesus' teaching? There are no one-size-fits-all regulations, love indeed having to decide afresh in each and every circumstance. It may seem woolly, but in fact it's the most demanding way of all, for it must meet people where they are rather than take refuge in moral certainties.

To illustrate what that means, I want to paint for you four simple scenarios, each leading into points for discussion concerning issues that are anything but simple.

Scenario 1

Jack walked cheerfully through the school gates, then froze in dismay as he spotted a group of youths loitering ahead. He'd come to know them all too well across the years, their repeated bullying having made his life a misery and cast a shadow over what should have been carefree times. Hurriedly he pressed himself against the wall and tried to sidle back the way he'd come, hoping he hadn't been noticed, but it was no good – the gang were advancing menacingly towards him, grinning as they approached.

Should he run? He wanted to, but what was the point? They'd catch him soon enough and punish him all the more for their exertions. So he just stood there, waiting for the fist in the stomach, the kick on the shin, the slap across the face, determined if nothing else to keep the tears from his eyes during his ritual humiliation.

They were upon him now, yet no fist came – no sickening thud and writhing on the floor in agony . . . nothing! Dimly he was aware of the ringleader speaking, and suddenly it dawned on Jack that the words were not of insult but apology and the outstretched hand a gesture of friendship rather than aggression. The most feared boy in the school – his name for so long a byword for brutality and aggression – was speaking of faith, remorse, and new beginnings; he who had shown no mercy now seeking forgiveness. Could it be true? Surely not! But Jack wasn't going to argue the toss. Hesitantly he shook the proffered hand, still expecting some sting in the tail, and when none came he raced off – baffled, bewildered, but, above all, relieved.

Discussion points

- Does that story seem a little far-fetched? You might think so, but you'd be wrong, for *I* was the one being bullied and the ringleader in question was literally transformed overnight, going on to become a full-time Christian evangelist! Can you think of other people who have changed as dramatically from an attitude of hate to love? Have you personally known anyone transformed in this way? Are there people you've given up on or do you still believe they can change?

- Few of us will experience such a radical transformation from hate to love, simply because we didn't actually hate in the first place, but is love more a part of your life now than it was before you became a Christian? Jesus spoke of loving one's enemy. Could you have done that in Jack's shoes?

- Jesus speaks of people knowing we're his disciples by our love. Is that realistic? Do you think people see a distinctive quality of love in your life? Do you think they see *any* love in your life?

Scenario 2

Private Taylor dived down into the crater as a shell exploded nearby, accompanied by yet another burst of machinegun fire. He couldn't take much more of this – hour upon hour grovelling in the mud waiting for the bullet or shard of shrapnel that would put an end to his war, maybe even his life, as it had done for so many of his colleagues. He'd seen hundreds cut down beside him, their bodies mangled beyond recognition, and the sights and sounds of battle, too dreadful for words, haunted his thoughts day and night. How he hated this place, and, most of all, how he hated the enemy who made it necessary for him to be there. If he could only get his hands on them, he'd make them pay.

A sudden moaning broke into his thoughts – animal-like, stomach-churning – the sound of someone in agony, piteously appealing for help. He turned reluctantly, fearful of what he might see . . . then gasped, in relief and shock. It wasn't one of his comrades, but a German, his face a welter of blood, an arm almost severed, and a tangle of shattered bones protruding from a gaping wound in his chest.

Suddenly all hatred was gone, replaced simply by compassion for a fellow human being in need. He took his hip flask of rum and put it to the lips of the stricken soldier, who drank urgently, desperate to numb the pain. Blinking back tears from his eyes, Taylor gently cradled the man's head in his arms, cursing now not the enemy but this foul and futile war. There was nothing he could do, nothing *anyone* could do, except offer what support he could as the life ebbed slowly away. The wounded man shuddered in a last paroxysm of pain, then looked up with a smile of gratitude before his eyes glazed over and looked out no more.

Discussion points

- What things stop you from loving others? Are there situations in which you fail to love as much as you should? Are you willing to enlarge on these?

- What does love in the Christian sense actually mean? What *doesn't* it mean? Does anything set apart the love Christians show to that shown by others? Do you think it should?

- Can love conquer hate or is this simply naïve idealism? Would you see the non-violent campaigns of Martin Luther King or Mahatma Gandhi, or the resistance of those like Desmond Tutu, Allan Boesak and Trevor Huddleston to apartheid in South Africa, as examples of love in action? If so, what do you make of the fact that Gandhi was a Hindu? Consider also the subsequent work of the Truth and Reconciliation Commission. What impact has this had and what might have happened without it?

Scenario 3

'It's not fair!' snarled Jason, glaring furiously at his mother.

'It's perfectly fair, dear,' she answered, 'as you well know.'

'It's not,' snapped Jason. 'Why can't I borrow the money if I want to? Gareth's dad allowed *him* to borrow even more.'

'Maybe he did, but that's not the point. For one thing, you can't afford to repay it and you certainly don't want a mountain of debt hanging round your neck. For another, I honestly think you'll be wasting your money and be far better spending it on something else. And anyway, you don't *deserve* it at the moment – not after that scrape you got yourself into, for which, may I remind you, your father and I are still having to pay.'

Jason, however, was having none of it. 'If you really loved me,' he muttered, 'you'd *give* me as much as I need. You just don't care, do you?'

'I *do* care,' sighed his mother, well used to his emotional blackmail, 'and that's precisely why the answer's still no. Giving in would be the easy option, but eventually it would do none of us any good. I'm not enjoying this, Jason, despite what you think, but it's because I love you so much that I won't change my mind. Hopefully you'll understand one day.'

But Jason wasn't ready to listen any longer. With a snort he got up and stormed out the room, slamming the door behind him.

Discussion points

- Are there times when love involves being cruel to be kind? Can you give examples? Have you experienced this firsthand?

- Do you see love as an easy or hard option? Can it be used as a way of sitting on the fence and avoiding complex moral issues or is the opposite true?

- Have there been times when love has led you to question biblical teaching or established church doctrine?

Scenario 4

The true story of Nicky Cruz will be familiar to many from the powerful 1970 film *The Cross and the Switchblade*. Brought up in Puerto Rico by parents steeped in witchcraft, Nicky was soon no stranger to trouble and when, in 1955, aged 16, he and his brother were sent to live in New York City, he quickly became part of the infamous Mau Maus gang, equally swiftly rising to become their leader. Street-fights, drug-taking, robbery and murder became a way of life for him until David Wilkerson, an itinerant preacher, began crusading in the ghetto, persevering with his mission despite Nicky beating him up and threatening to kill him if he continued. When Wilkerson hired a hall in the area for an evangelistic rally, Cruz decided to make good his threat, but when he arrived at the scene and heard Wilkerson preaching, something came over him, and instead of attacking the preacher he knelt down and prayed, asking forgiveness from both Wilkerson and God. He went on to train for the ministry, returning to the ghettoes to win for Christ many of his old gang, including their new leader. The founder of Nicky Cruz Outreach, devoted to helping troubled young people, and of 'halfway houses' aimed at the rehabilitation of drug addicts, Cruz has preached the gospel across the world.

Discussion points

- Can you think of other people who have been shining examples of love? What was it that motivated them?

- Are Christians meant to love everyone? Is this possible in the real world? Is there a danger of sentimentalising, offering pious platitudes? Could you, for example, feel love for a terrorist, murderer or rapist?

- Has the Church/religion been an agency for love or hatred across the years? Does this raise issues that Christianity and we as Christians need to face?

Food for thought

Consider the following proverbs and quotations. What are they saying? Which do you find most helpful? What are their strengths and weaknesses? Do you agree or disagree with the point they're making?

- Love cures people – both the ones who give it and the ones who receive it. (Carl Menninger)

- Give me such love for God and men, as will blot out all hatred and bitterness. (Dietrich Bonhoeffer)

- I have decided to stick with love. Hate is too great a burden to bear. (Martin Luther King)

- People are lonely because they build walls instead of bridges. (J. F. Newton)

- If I love the world as it is, I am already changing it. A first fragment of the world has been changed, and that is my own heart. (Petru Dumitriu)

- Love is the movement, effusion and advancement of the heart toward the good. (St Francis de Sales)

- Have a heart that never hardens, and a temper that never tires, and a touch that never hurts. (Charles Dickens)

- Only love can bring individual beings to their perfect completion as individuals because only love takes possession of them and unites them by what lies deepest within them. (Teilhard de Chardin)

- Where there is no love, pour love in, and you will draw out love. (St John of the Cross)

- To love is to wish the other's highest good. (R. H. Benson)

- I beg you to stamp everything with the seal of love, nothing else will last. (Elizabeth of the Trinity)

- We have just enough religion to make us hate, but not enough to make us love one another. (Jonathan Swift)

- Love seeks one thing only: the good of the one loved. It leaves all the other secondary effects to take care of themselves. Love, therefore, is its own reward. (Thomas Merton)

- Love is all we have, the only way that each can help the other. (Euripides)

- Some day, after mastering the winds, the waves, the tides, and gravity, we shall harness for God the energies of love, and then, for the second time in the history of the world, man will have discovered fire. (Teilhard de Chardin)

Prayer

You make it sound so simple, Lord,
 summarising the Law and the Prophets,
 the way to life itself,
 in one simple command:
 to love.
But we don't find it simple at all.
We find it harder than we ever imagined,
 both understanding what love involves,
 and then acting upon it.

When we are faced with complex situations,
 and are unsure what love asks of us,
 afraid we may hurt instead of heal,
 harm instead of help,
 teach us your way,
 the way of love incarnate.

When love is demanding,
 calling for sacrifices we would rather not make,
 choices we would prefer to ignore,
 commitment we are reluctant to give,
 a response that goes against the grain,
 teach us your way,
 the way of love incarnate.

When we find others hard to love,
 our attitude towards them clouded by hurt, jealousy,
 pride and anger,
 so much that poisons relationships,
 teach us your way,
 the way of love incarnate.

When we are indifferent to others,
 so wrapped up in our own world,

our own concerns and interests,
that we overlook their needs,
teach us your way,
the way of love incarnate.

When our words say one thing but our lives say another,
our talk of a special kind of love
belied by the mediocrity of our discipleship,
the lack of anything even remotely distinctive,
teach us your way,
the way of love incarnate.
Amen.

Completing the picture

Below are some biblical verses exploring God's call to love. Reflect on them quietly together and then discuss any further thoughts arising from them.

- If I speak in the tongues of people or angels, but do not have love, I become nothing more than a blasting trumpet or clashing cymbal. If I have the gift of prophecy and understand all mysteries and all knowledge, and if I have faith such as to remove mountains, yet do not have love, then I am nothing. If I dispense all my goods and surrender my body to be burned, yet do not have love, it profits me nothing. Love is patient and kind; it is not jealous or puffed up with its own importance, vaunting itself before others, nor does it knowingly cause offence. It does not seek its own well-being, is not easily provoked, and does not think evil or rejoice in wrongdoing but rejoices rather in the truth. It embraces all things, believes all things, hopes all things, endures all things. Love is eternal. Three things continue – faith, hope and love – and the greatest of them is love. (1 Corinthians 13:1-8a, 13)

- You have become a new person, your minds being renewed into the likeness of the one who created you. So then, as God's chosen ones, holy and greatly loved, clothe yourselves with compassion, kindness, humility, meekness and patience, being merciful to one another and forgiving any quarrel you may have; in other words, forgive as the Lord forgave you. Above all, clothe yourselves with love, which binds everything together in perfect harmony. (Colossians 3:9b, 10, 12-14)

- My advice to you is to love your enemies, do good to those who hate you, and pray for whoever mistreats you. Do for others precisely what you'd like them to do to you. Why should you expect a blessing for loving only those who love you? Even sinners do that. (Luke 6:27, 28, 31, 32)

Blessing

Gracious God,
    may your love fill us,
    transform us,
    sustain us
    and flow through us,
    this day and always.
Amen.

Summary of sessions

Session 1: Called to serve – Jonah 1:1-3

- A God who calls
- A God who wants to communicate with us
- A God of justice
- A God who gives us free will

Extracts from Jonah's Journal

An unwanted calling

Received an unexpected wake-up call today. All set for a lie-in, but God had other plans. Can you believe it? He wanted me to go to Nineveh, to tell the people there that they had been really wicked – in the proper sense of the word.

'That's going to make me very popular, isn't it?' I argued.

'No need for sarcasm,' God replied.

So we left it like that – sort of *in the air*!

Making my escape

Came up with a brilliant plan last night: I'm going to run away! What do you think about that? All my bags are packed. By the time God comes looking for me, I'll be gone. He'll never find me – not where I'm going. Anyway, must go, I've got a boat to catch at Joppa. Bon voyage!

Answers to activities

Session 1

The eleven differences are as follows:

Pattern on flag	Number of birds
Time on clock	Door handles on main door
Shape of side door	Door handle on lean-to door
Bars on lean-to window	Person's arms
Horizontal bar on nave window	Roof tiles
Position and shape of cloud	